Read what they are saying about . . .

The Two Minute Motivator
How to Inspire Superior Performance

"Congratulations! You have done it again. ***The Two Minute Motivator*** cuts through the latest fad theories and presents it's concepts in a efficient and simplified manner. Managers will want to read this book again and again."

Frank A. Smola, President
Merlin's Muffler and Brake

"***The Two Minute Motivator*** is an easy to follow, common sense approach to inspiring employees. Why can't all management be this easy to understand?"

Jeanne Larson, Manager
Regional Marketing/Customer Service
NIKE

"This book is great! *The Two Minute Motivator* puts into words what it takes years to develop and implement."

>Jackie Meyers, Manager
>Human Resources
>The Gates Rubber Company

"*The Two Minute Motivator* is a thought provoking read which pleasantly consumed an 850 mile plane ride. You've successfully mapped out an easily applied process to stimulate employees through improved communications. Your principles are sound and worth employing. I'll be sure to share it with my peers."

>Timothy M. Richards, Manager
>Sales Development
>General Electric Company

"Congratulations on a great book. With change in the work place accelerating, motivation is of paramount importance. *The Two Minute Motivator* is right on target."

>Robert W. Gras, Vice President/CFO
>International and Business Development Group
>US WEST

"Good things come in small packages, only this time they are in a wonderful little book called ***The Two Minute Motivator.*** Thanks Bob! I can appreciate the concise writing about a topic we all need to work on continuously."

      Leo Perino, Director
      Human Resources
  Western Farm Bureau Management Corporation

"The Two Minute Motivator is common sense management for a common sense world."

      Gail Forsyth, Manager
  "Your Idea/Your Universe" Suggestion Program
   AT&T Universal Card Services Corporation

"With the labor force changing the way it is, ***The Two Minute Motivator*** will put you several steps ahead of the pack when it comes to motivating employees."

     Allan Sterbin, Director
    HR Selection and Evaluation
    The Promus Companies
(Hampton Inns, Embassy Suites, Homewood Inns)

The Two Minute Motivator:
How to Inspire Superior Performance

Copyright 1992 by Robert W. Wendover

Management Staff Press, Inc.
7500 E. Arapahoe Road
Englewood, CO 80112
1-800-227-5510

ISBN 0-9623289-1-X

Library of Congress # 92-080076

Wendover, Robert Warren, 1955 -
   The Two Minute Motivator: how to inspire superior performance/
Robert W. Wendover

   p. cm.
   0-9623289-1-X

   1. Employee Motivation. 2. Psychology, Industrial. I. Title.
II. Title: How to inspire superior performance. III. Title: The 2
minute motivator.

HF5549.5.M63W4 1992   658.314
                              QBI-179

All rights reserved. No part of this publication may be reproduced, stored in a retrieval system, or transmitted, in any form or by any means, electronic, mechanical, photocopying, recording, or otherwise, without the prior written permission of the copyright owner.

Printed in the United States of America

Dedication

To you, who strive valiantly for innovative ways to motivate those in the work place. May this book be a source of inspiration for years to come.

Books by Robert W. Wendover

Smart Hiring:
The Complete Guide for Recruiting Employees

High Performance Hiring

The Two Minute Motivator:
How to Inspire Superior Performance

Contents

Introduction 1

The Secrets of Two Minute Motivation 4

Uncovering Employees' Hidden Motivations 32

Exploring Your Values and Motivations 58

Inspiring Motivation in Others 88

Putting the Two Minute Motivator to Work 104

Acknowledgements 125

About the author 126

 *Introduction*

Motivation. Productivity. Self-esteem. The success of any organization rests on these three concepts. But why are some managers better at this skill than others? What does it take to motivate those you lead?

Understanding what lies behind the actions people take and the things they believe is essential to inspiring them. ***The Two Minute Motivator*** will enable you to better determine what motivates your employees.

If you are a new manager, you'll learn how to turn your theories about motivation into practical application. If you have supervised people before, this book will help you gain even deeper insight in to how to inspire each individual and turn them into top performers. You'll discover what they need in you as a leader and you'll discover specific ways to regain your employees' trust, dedication and commitment to their jobs.

No one excels in their relationships without the help and support of others. What you do with what you observe along with how you act determines your own success. It is simple to say that you must observe and respond to the behavior of others. As a process, that is all it takes. But polishing your observation skills and refining your actions is what this book is about.

In an age of frantic schedules and hurried decisions, it is easy to overlook the obvious keys to inspiring the performance of others. Too often managers take their employees' existence for granted and fail to give them the individualized attention they deserve.

Yet, by dedicating yourself to being a better observer and to be more committed to treating others as unique individuals, you will make great strides in inspiring your people to exceed your own expectations of them.

This is not just a business book. This is also a people book. These principles apply at home, on the playing field, in your place of worship and in all your personal and professional associations.

The Two Minute Motivator is not simply a two minute activity. It is a series of two-minute opportunities which will help you better understand others -- their biases and behaviors -- and will give you specific strategies for dealing with them effectively. You'll learn how to arouse better productivity and increased morale by applying these principles.

Read this book, and re-frame your approach to motivating those with whom you work every day. Grasp the concepts and discover abundant new ways for inspiring outstanding performance.

The Secrets of Two Minute Motivation

Motivating people is not a complicated, time-consuming process. It does however, require keen observation skills and the ability to organize the information you gather about others. Every person's motivation is a result of their experiences, perceptions and attitudes.

If you manage or supervise others, you know how difficult it is to find the right keys to motivation. Inspiring others to do a good job may seem to elude you a great deal of the time. Remember . . .

You cannot force other people to be motivated. But you can provide the stimulus for them to motivate themselves.

If you want to encourage co-workers to improve the quality of their work for instance, you must first understand how they perceive the work they do. Each individual reveals their attitudes by using *self-talk*.

What is *self-talk*? It's the voice you use to talk to yourself as you go through your day. Whether you are aware of it or not, you are constantly asking yourself questions, expressing your opinions or giving yourself warnings. What you say to yourself is a result of the information you already have stored about a great number of subjects.

If you are trying to decide between two products for example, your self-talk might be saying, "The red one's really nice, but the blue one goes better with my car . . ." This internal voice helps you decide which product to choose based on what preferences and opinions you already have about the colors, red and blue.

At other times, your self-talk may reveal

questions you have about a problem or issue. As you read this, your self-talk might be saying, "What is he talking about?"

In response, you might say to yourself, "I don't talk to myself... do I?" and realize that you are doing it right now! We can never get away from this continuous process we use to talk to ourselves.

Everybody uses self-talk: your friends, co-workers, boss and spouse. These little conversations help reveal the attitudes you have about every topic and every person you encounter.

So, in order to motivate your employees, you must first examine their attitudes, or what they are saying to themselves. If an employee is making assumptions based on incorrect or insufficient information, then their attitudes may lead them to jump to incorrect conclusions or to take the wrong actions.

Employees who are de-motivated often base their attitudes and actions on incorrect or incomplete information. In order to motivate them, you must give these employees enough correct information to change their self-talk into something more positive. This will, in turn help your employees to make more reasonable decisions.

If you want to motivate an unenthusiastic office worker for instance, you must understand what that person is saying to themselves. On one hand, the employee may be saying, "this job is so boring, I'm going to go out of my mind!" On the other hand, they may be saying, "I haven't the faintest idea what I'm doing. Maybe if I do as little as possible, I won't get into trouble."

Obviously, the employee's self-talk is very different in each of these instances. It is crucial that you discover what employees are saying to themselves. That way you can determine how to motivate this individual. In one case, the worker may need more challenges, in the other, additional job skills may be necessary.

The only way to find out which scenario in

these two scenarios is true of this employee's case is to observe, ask and listen. Very few employees will take the initiative to approach their boss and say, "I'm bored" or "I'm in over my head."

The comments an employee makes in the office, during meetings or to others over lunch can provide valuable keys to the nature of their self-talk. How they act, the decisions they make and their quality of work can also help you understand what going on inside their head.

If you take these observations and add them to the information you already know about this worker (such as work history, education, and level of confidence), you will develop a detailed picture of how you can best motivate them. You'll be able to encourage your employees' productivity and satisfaction on the job.

✻ ✻ ✻

* * *

You can't motivate other people . . .

But you can provide the stimulus for them to motivate themselves!

* * *

Gathering these insights does not happen overnight. You gain more understanding over time. The observations you make and the bits of information you discover about your employees come as a result of talking and listening to them in two or three minute opportunities from time to time.

During these chances to interact, you have the opportunity to coach, encourage or challenge them to do a better job. Hence the title of this book: ***The Two Minute Motivator.***

The Two Minute Motivator can help you reframe the way you motivate others. Using two minute opportunities will prove so effective that soon they will become habits you incorporate into your daily management style. You don't have the time to sit down with each employee for an hour to figure out what makes them tick. You must accomplish this through observing and interacting with your employees repeatedly, but for just minutes at a time.

You can apply the principles in this book in the frantic pace of today's world. The amount of work you must accomplish each day often requires you to react quickly to the situations you face. If you don't take charge of the way you motivate your employees, you will lose your opportunity to steer them to greater productivity and higher self-esteem.

It's easy to assume that every leader wants to get better at motivating their employees. But following through on those desires to improve your skills is a different matter.

It is easy to become distracted by other priorities and place employees' need for guidance on a back burner. Without consistency however, keeping people inspired becomes an impossible task.

People tend to think of themselves first. Because of this, many supervisors make the mistake of assuming others think and feel the same way. This means that a supervisor may falsely believe that their people are all motivated that same way they are.

If the supervisor forces their likes and dislikes on these other people, the effort to motivate them will fail.

* * *

*Never assume your people
see a situation
the same way you see it!*

* * *

Listen to what your employees talk about with passion. What inspires you may completely turn off someone else. Your love of sports for instance, may discourage another person from wanting to interact with you because they perceive you as a "jock." Just the same, you may believe that those who bury themselves in books or academic study are boring. To be a good motivator, you must develop the ability to keep your values separate from those of your co-workers. When you do, you will be well on your way to finding the best ways to motivate others.

Above all, you must be consistent and sincere when trying to motivate others. The way you communicate with employees reveals your own internal beliefs. If others suspect you are being insincere to them, not only will you fail to motivate them but, in fact, you will discourage them.

Your employees care about how you treat them. They also notice how you treat others. If you show favoritism or dislike to anyone, these behaviors will discourage employees from trusting you.

Being consistent in the way you react to each person means treating everone fairly. You must be consistent in the amount of time you talk and listen to each person, in the way you reward and discipline, and in your overall management style to demonstrate your desire to be fair.

Using two minute opportunities to inspire your employees demonstrates your trust, consistency, caring and understanding. People who believe they are trusted, cared for and understood, will not only meet, but exceed your expectations.

People have a way of rising or falling to meet other people's expectations of them. Your ability to instill the desire in your employees to satisfy your high expectations will help determine your success in getting outstanding performance.

Building a productive team is impossible unless you recognize the differences in how each person is motivated. You are leading a diverse group of people. Your ability to build a team out of those individuals depends on your skill in recognizing each team member's individuality.

Motivating others means constantly recognizing and acknowledging what your employees are contributing to the cause. If you are inconsis-

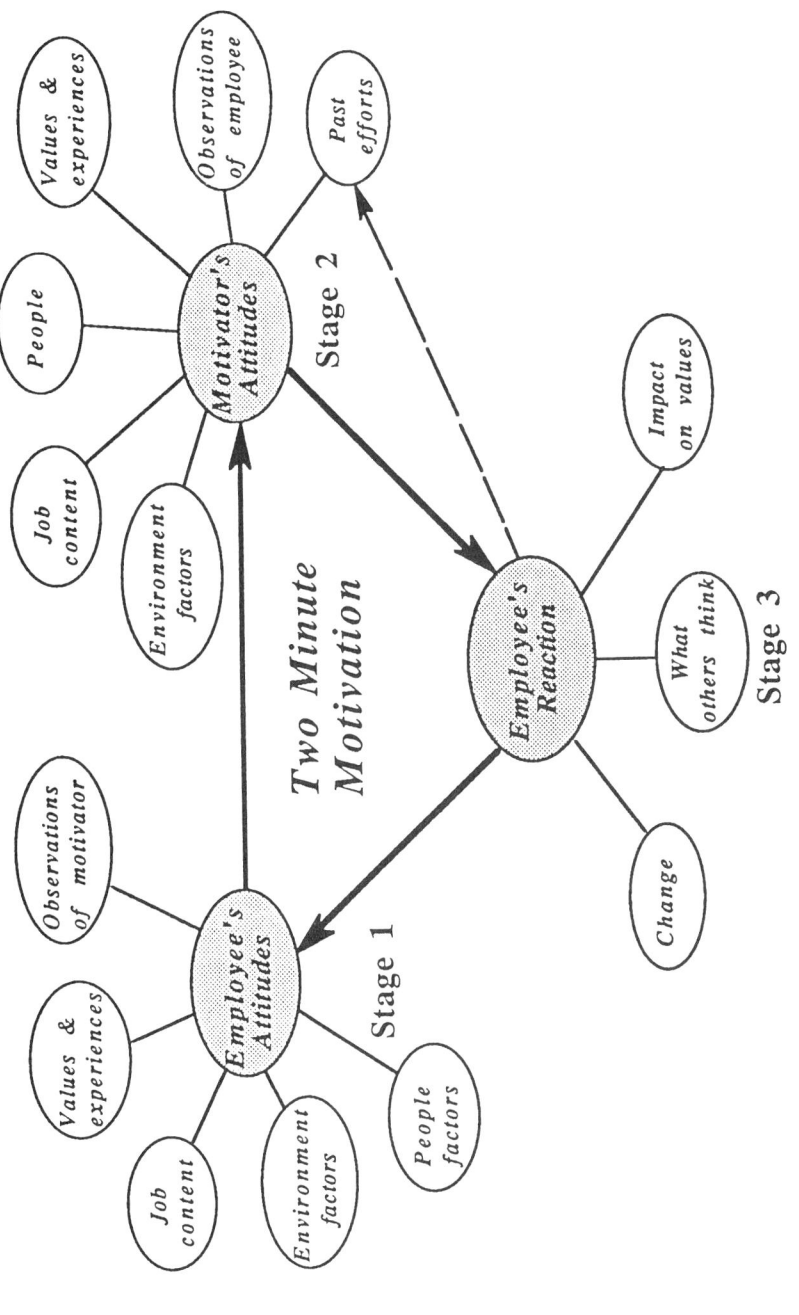

tent in the way you motivate your people, they will respond with a lack of effort and diminished productivity.

Understanding Two Minute Motivation

The *Two Minute Motivator* process consists of three stages. A diagram of the process is on page 15.

The first stage is to consider the individual's actions and attitudes as they are revealed to you in the work place. These actions and attitudes help you determine the person's values, level of self-esteem, understanding of their job, past experience, and how they respond to both the work environment and to others in the organization.

The second stage is to consider how your actions and attitudes influence your ability to motivate other people. Your actions and attitudes are based on values, experience, self-esteem, and understanding of your job. You are also influenced by your observations of the individual, work environment, other people in the organiztion and the results of your past efforts to motivate that person.

The third stage is that person's reaction to your attempts to motivate them. How they react depends on the person's ability to cope with change, what they believe other people will think, and how well your action meets their needs and corresponds to their values.

After your employee reacts, you must make a mental note of how they responded so you can later evaluate how effective you were in motivating them. (Dotted line in the diagram..)

The key to using *Two Minute Motivation* is to stick to the two minute format. These short time intervals provide repeated opportunities to better understand your employees and to steer them in a positive direction. A couple of examples might help.

No. 1: You overhear someone discussing the difficulty they are having learning a new set of product codes. While you don't want to interrupt the conversation, you take note of what is being said to use for future reference.

In this example, the second step is to spend a short amount of time talking and listening to your employee and trying to understand what you can do to meet their needs.

You might engage them in a conversation about product codes at the coffee stand for instance. During that discussion, you may teach them a quick game you used to play with yourself for remembering the codes and their meanings.

The third step is to assess your employee's reaction to your attempt to motivate them. In this example, they will consider how comfortable they will feel with your suggestion. They might consider what others will think of them when they are playing the game or they may wonder whether the game makes sense to them.

At this stage, you will want to note your employee's change, or lack of change, in behavior. They may play the game and learn the codes, and their motivation may go up. If they resist the game, their motivation will either remain the same or decrease.

In either case you, as the motivator, must make a mental note of your employee's response for future reference.

No. 2: The work of a long time employee has been slipping over the past two months. They have also become more arrogant in the way they respond to co-workers. While no one has said anything to you, you can detect a level of tension whenever this person is in the work area.

The *first step* is to examine the values, attitudes and background of this person. They have been an employee longer than anyone else in the department. In fact, you learned a great deal from them when you took the position, even though you were the manager.

They have been through the automation that took place five years ago, not to mention the hassle with the new telephone system that almost put the company under. They have probably trained half the people in your department because you didn't have the time.

In truth, everyone in the department should be thankful this person is around, yet about two months ago they proposed a new system at the staff meeting that was immediately shot down by everyone else. There was nothing wrong with the plan. In fact, it would improve overall customer service. But it was obvious that it would mean additional work and no one was in favor of that.

Ever since that meeting, this person has been arrogant and sometimes, downright caustic with other employees. Lately, this person has been prefacing everything they say with, "You weren't around then. But the way we used to do it was . . ." Maybe that's a signal that they felt put down by the newer employees.

The *second step* is to examine your own motives and feelings in relation to this person. How you feel about them is going to have an impact on how you try to motivate them.

When you first began supervising them, you were a little intimidated since they knew the systems and you didn't. But after a few uncomfortable encounters, you finally resolved your feelings and they have supported you ever since.

You respect and admire their contribution to the department. Yet when they came up with a good idea, you let the other employees defeat it without giving the idea a good hearing. They probably felt abandoned in the meeting. After the meeting, they may have decided to stop making suggestions if they were going to fall on deaf ears.

Now it's up to you to find a way to remotivate this person and encourage their contribution. But you want to do it discreetly.

The third step in *Two Minute Motivation* is to develop and implement ways to motivate the person. You might begin by bringing up their original idea in conversation.

You might say, "What ever happened to that idea about servicing customers you had a couple of months ago? I kind of liked it."

Wait for their reaction. If it is hostile, ("You ought to know. You let it get shot down in a meeting.") then you'll need to try a different approach. If they seem open to the idea of discussing it, look for ways to build support for it in the department.

You might bring it up at a staff meeting and give this person a lot of credit. If other employees try to shoot it down, go to bat for it. Ask why they are so against it. Do they have a better solution? Even if the idea is not implemented, this person will see that you are suporting them.

Find other ways to recognize this person. Encourage them to contribute and work to ease the tension between them and other employees. If their work continues to slip, then you will need to discuss it. But this can be done without the confrontation the earlier situation may have caused.

Throughout this process, make notes on what worked to motivate them and what didn't. Chances are, you'll need to motivate them again.

The Three Keys to Two Minute Motivation

The first key to inspiring outstanding performance is to know your own values. Your values influence everything you do and think. How effective you are with anyone or any group depends on how well you understand what influences you.

Motivation is not just a top-down process. Everything you experience with others is filtered through the screen of your own experiences and biases. Exploring your own values is critical to understanding the values and motivations of others.

The second key to inspiring outstanding performance is to recognize how diverse people are. It's very tempting to stereotype people in many ways We tend to take a broad-brush approach, and conclude that all those with a particular similarity respond the same way.

While deep down we may know that stereotypes are far too general in nature, it is easier to assume these generalizations than to make the effort to pay close attention to the character of each individual separately.

Using a broad-brush approach works against us by sending the message that we do not care for individual differences. Your ability to individually tailor your actions to each person with whom you come in contact, is a key to inspiring them.

Each person is a unique combination of experiences and heredity. Even identical twins vary significantly in their actions and attitudes. Those able to ferret out these differences will be rewarded with trust, caring and understanding.

The third key is to recognize the value of these individual diversities. What can you do to help those you work with to take advantage of the diverse strengths of others in the workplace.

A person with an American Indian heritage for instance, might be the best person to deal with a difficult customer with a similar background.

In another situation, you may find that a veteran may be the best choice to approach military accounts. The fact that they understand the "military" way of thinking puts the customer's mind at ease and helps them to find common points of communication.

While you must be careful of stereotypes and myths, recognizing a co-worker's strength in dealing with a particular situation demonstrates that you value that worker as a person rather than just another employee.

Simply celebrating an employee's personal accomplishment outside of the workplace shows your concern for their well-being. The value of recognition goes a long way toward building long-term motivation in every individual.

Individual diversity includes many things. To understand these differences, begin by making a list of your employees' physical characteristics. You will include traits such as age, height, physical appearance, weight, attire, skin and hair color. Continue by writing down their skill levels in various job-related activities, their formal education and the training they have received since they began the job they have now.

Consider each person's work, social, and military experience, family background, nationality, economic situation, and sexual orientation. These, among other factors, combine to form a complex picture of each person with whom you work and interact.

But before you explore what influences other people, take a look at yourself. How do you think other people see you? Understanding the way you affect other people is a vital link in motivating them.

If you don't know how your employees perceive you, ask them. However, make sure you do so in a way that encourages honest feedback. Your employees must know that you will not penalize them for whatever information they tell you.

Motivation begins with understanding the individual, but it extends beyond this point. Other factors must be taken into consideration. Consider your environment. Think about the policies, schedules, pace, physical layout and other characteristics which color it. How do these things work together to inspire outstanding performance? How do they hinder performance?

Consider the corporate attitude at your company. By simply walking through a work environment, most people can get a clear feeling of the general attitude of the people who work there. How do people get along with each other? Is there an atmosphere of caring and cooperation? Or one upmanship?? Does the group, as a whole, desire success?

Finally, consider how the people in general respond to change. Is change mostly positive or negative? Trying to motivate someone who is afraid of change requires a different approach than someone who welcomes change and sees it as more of an opportunity. The same holds true with a group. You must be prepared to address the group's apprehensions. How has change taken place in the past? How do they respond to different types of changes? Successful change can be very motivating. Unsuccessful change can be debilitating. You must pave the way for making changes positive by listening to your people's comments and concerns and taking them into account. Motivation cannot be forced. Even if you feel a person needs to be motivated, they may not necessarily agree. By observing them, you can determine their attitude toward change and motivation.

* * *

In summary, tailoring what you do to meet your people's needs is the key ingredient to finding the best way to motivate them. Each person has their own set of values, ideals, and emotions. Simply insisting they accept your values, ideals and emotions will result in de-motivated employees.

Two Minute Motivation will help you inspire those around you to outstanding performance and greater job satisfaction. For the most part, good leaders are aware of the principles we have identified. What are you doing to stimulate enthusiasm, commitment and high self-esteem in the people you deal with daily?

As you use the two minute concept we have discussed in this chapter, you will be able to respond to each person in your organization as a unique individual.

Remember the three stages of motivation:

1. Consider your employees' attitiudes before to try to motivate them.

2. Think about your own attitudes and behavior and try to keep them from negatively influencing your attempt to motivate employees.

3. Evaluate how your employees react to your attempts to motivate them. Keep this information in mind to use the next time you interact with each individual.

In the next four chapters, you will learn specific ways in which you can use these simple techniques to inspire outstanding performance in those you manage.

* * *

The **Two Minute Motivator** remembers that:

1. The keys to **Two Minute Motivation** are observation and action.

2. You cannot motivate people. You can only provide the stimulus for people to motivate themselves.

3. To understand how a person thinks, you must tap into their self-talk.

4. De-motivated people are basing their actions on incorrect or incomplete information.

5. To motivate someone, you must anticipate their attitude and behaviors.

6. Motivation must be consistent and tailored to every staff member.

7. People will rise or fall to meet your expectations.

* * *

Inspired employees

are happier employees.

* * *

 **Uncovering Employees' Hidden Motivations**

Where do people's attitudes and values come from? How do their beliefs affect their sense of motivation?

Every individual has a different set of experiences. That person's perceptions of the work place are based on those experiences. In trying to motivate them, it is your job to discover which variables impact each person within your organization and how these variables affect their behavior.

The information you gather about each person will provide you with valuable insight into what motivates them at work. This information includes personal elements such as the person's age, education, and work experience. But it also includes less subjective elements such as what the job is, the nature of the work environment and the personalities of co-workers.

No one wants to psychoanalyze those who report to them. But as a supervisor, you must filter your attempts to motivate them through the observations you have made of that person's performance and attitudes. While the elements just mentioned are constantly present, different ones affect the person's decisions and emotions at different times.

A staff member may respond positively to you most of the time. Yet they may become obstinate when a particular co-worker is in the room. This lack of cooperation might be tied directly to some bad feelings they have about that co-worker. Having observed this reaction, you might make a mental note not to attempt to motivate this person when that co-worker is in the room.

In another situation, you might notice that a staff member leaves the room whenever one or more smokers enter it. Based on this insight, you

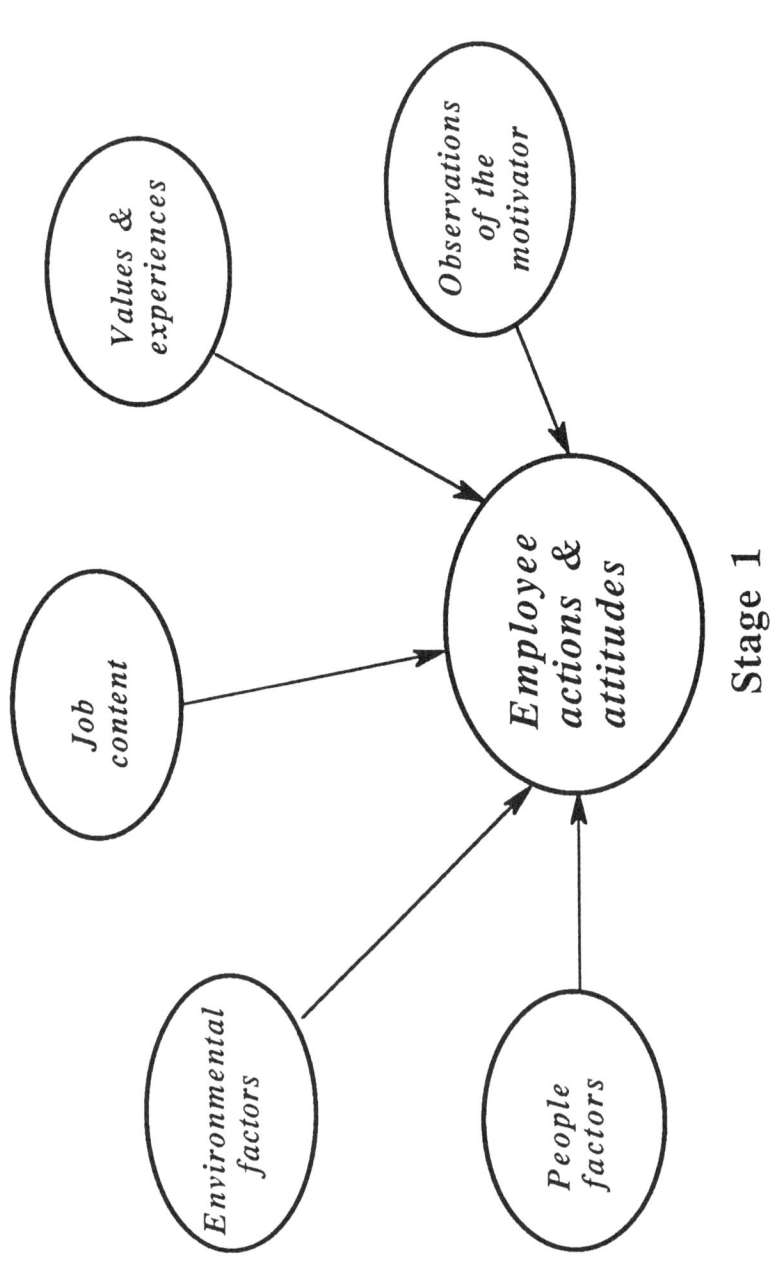

may be able to improve this person's productivity by providing them with a smoke-free work area. If, on the other hand, you decide to eliminate smoking from the work place, consider what impact that will have on the smokers' motivation.

Factors Affecting Worker Motivation

As you can see from the diagram on page 34, there are a host of elements that impact how a person reacts on the job. Some might be considered *internal* factors such as the person's values and background. Others may be considered *external* such as the work environment and job content. Each of these factors influences the motivation of each employee.

Let's take a look at each one and how they impact the people you manage:

External factors

Job content: What the job is all about is central to how people view their existence within the organization. Therefore, it is critical that they feel comfortable doing the job every day.

Many people who fail in a position do so because they have difficulty developing the skills and understanding of what the job actually requires. This feeling of inadequacy leads to feelings of frustration and lowered productivity. If the situation is not resolved, it can lead to anger and eventually termination or resignation.

For example, if a retail clerk seems to be making an unreasonable number of mistakes, it may mean he is having difficulty understanding the new computerized cash registers. You may have thoroughly trained him on the new system. But a little encouragement and review may be just what the person needs. While this advice may sound like common sense, do you follow it as often as you can?

A critical part of any motivator's job is to determine how well each person on their staff understands the job.

Work *environment:* While being able to adequately define their job is critical, a healthy, stimulating work environment is also important. A person's work includes everything in their physical surroundings such as lighting, color of paint on the walls, number and location of windows and the size of each individual's work area.

It also includes the general work pace, noise level and neatness (or sloppiness) of the working environment. There are also more subtle factors which influence people's perceptions of their place of work. Among other things, this includes the reliability of the copier and other office machines, availability of supplies and how easily someone can figure out the telephone system.

All of these factors, plus many more, combine to create an atmosphere that affects different people in different ways. While some people might adjust well to a messy work area for instance, it might send others into a frenzy.

Overall frustrations such as an unreliable copy machine can be a real drag on morale. ("I wish they would just fix the blessed thing!")

People factors: Every person who works for an organization impacts everyone else. Those who survive best are the people who can adjust to and accept a variety of co-workers.

As you progress through each day, keep an eye out for actions and comments that give you clues about how people interact with each other. Who gets along with whom? Which people are pals? Which personalities are more outgoing? Who keeps more to themselves? And which employees are natural leaders among those you supervise?

In addition to noting what's generally going on in these personal relationships, consider the factors already mentioned such as the pace of activity, noise and stress level. By taking a step back to see the big picture, you'll have much better information for directing your motivational efforts.

For instance, one of your employees may prefer a quiet setting in which to concentrate. Another may thrive in a more lively environment where people yell ideas back and forth. Taking the time to discover which employees prefer what particular working environment will help you find the most effective ways to motivate them.

Each of these external factors impacts your employee's overall desire to contribute and share in the work place. These elements also contribute to their self-talk — or what people are saying to themselves while they work.

Internal factors

In addition to the external elements which influence motivation, people are also affected by internal elements. These include their personal values, level of education, degree of self-esteem and their feelings toward you, as their supervisor.

These internal factors have a significant impact on your employees' self-concepts. Their self-concept in turn, has a bearing on their level of motivation. As you know, a person's mood and their self-concept vary from day to day and even hour to hour.

It is your job as a motivator, to observe each person's actions and comments in order to detect how they might best be motivated at a given time.

Values and Background:

A person's values and background can be divided into three categories each of which contain several components:
Experience
Heritage
Physical factors

Experience includes the following:

Work: What jobs has this person held? In what industries? How well did they do in these positions? What successes or failures have they had? How long did they stay in their previous positions? Why did they leave? What are their career goals? How long have they been in their current position?

Education: What formal education has the person had? High school? Trade school? College? Graduate school? Any specialities?

Marital status: Is the person married? Divorced? What is their spouse like? What does their spouse do? Do they appear to have a healthy relationship?

Parental status: Does the employee have children? How many? How old? What are the children like?

Income: What is the employee's salary history? How much do they make now? Do these wages seem fair for the person's job level? How do the wages compare to those of their peers? Do they appear to live within their means? If not, how much do they seem to spend? Does this person have financial concerns?

Military experience: Is the person a veteran? What branch? Where were they stationed and what did they do? What rank? Which years did they serve? Does the employee have any issues or concerns about their past military experience?

Hobbies and sports activities: What hobbies do your co-workers enjoy? How enthusiastic are they about them? How often do they talk about their personal interests? Are these interests related related to their job? Are their hobbies used as a healthy or unhealthy way to escape?

The second category which influences a person's values and background is **heritage.** This category includes some sensitive issues. Therefore it is wise to be careful when asking questions so others are not offended. These may include the employee's religious and political beliefs, along with their racial background.

Be very careful however when gathering this information not to misuse it. While knowing as much as possible about your people can help you lead them better, they must be treated as distinct individuals. Stereotypes must be avoided at all costs.

* * *

Avoid stereotyping

at all costs!

* * *

Heritage includes:

Religious beliefs: Does your employee attend a place of worship? Which one? How involved are they? Do they feel comfortable sharing their beliefs? Do co-workers accept this?

Political beliefs: What are the person's political beliefs? How strong are they? Are they affiliated with a particular party? Do they regularly talk about them? How do their co-workers respond to the person's political leanings?

Race: What race is this individual (Black, White, Hispanic, Asian, etc.)? Do they exhibit any stereotypical attitudes or behaviors that may correspond to their ethnic background? Take a good look at your own stereotypes to see if they are valid. How are they viewed by co-workers?

Ethnicity: What is this person's nationality? How do they relate to their heritage? Do they feel comfortable discussing it? How do you know?

Sexual orientation: Is this person male or female? Do they seem comfortable talking about gender related issues? Or are such topics to be avoided? How do they generally feel about both men and women?

Geographic location: Where did this person grow up? Do they carry any conscious stereotypes about the region they are from? How proud are they about their geographical roots.

The third category influencing a person's values and background are ***physical factors:***
These include:

Age: How old is this person? How does their age compare with the rest of the employees? Are there general stereotypes about age you see expressed by this person? Are there others in the organization who have particular attitudes about age? Are there mandatory retirement policies?

Physical and mental abilities: Is this person able-bodied? If not, what kind of limitations do they experience? Are they sensitive about any of their physical attributes (weight, appearance, height, etc.)?

These values and background factors can play a critical role in helping you discover what motivates the individuals you lead.

Observations about you, their supervisor: The final factor you must consider about your employees' attitudes is how they feel about you, their supervisor. Like it or not, you are a role model for everyone else in the organization. Your actions and comments are analyzed by every member of your team and they influence how your people feel about their jobs.

You will probably find those who disagree with your point of view harder to motivate because they will be looking for flaws in you, your actions and your decisions. On the other hand, those who see most things your way will generally strive to support you.

Your ability to determine how each person you manage feels about you will help you conclude which motivational strategies will work for each of them. While motivation is still a series of trials and errors, predicting your employees' behavior in advance will give you an advantage in inspiring them.

For each individual, all the factors we've mentioned combine to form their level of self-esteem on the job. This self-esteem varies from day to day depending on circumstances related and unrelated to the work place. It is essential that you learn to adjust your behavior to your employees' varying moods and personal concerns.

An employee might be feeling very good about their job for instance, but a disagreement with their spouse may hinder them from doing their best that day at work. Your skill at detecting these changes in mood and finding ways to get your employee back on track will help determine the overall productivity and level of self-esteem of your workers.

* * *

An essential key to using *two minute motivation* is be able to grasp the opportunity to ask questions that will help you identify each individual's values and desires.

Having a two minute conversation with two employees about a particular project for instance, may help you discover that one person particularly enjoys creative tasks and another prefers detail work. Knowing this about each of them enables you to carefully tailor their projects in the future thereby producing better productivity and motivation in each.

If you are in touch with a person's values, you can anticipate their responses, actions and emotions. In other words, get to know your co-workers! Being pro-active in motivating them is a critical element in inspiring superior performance.

Motivation is not something that is turned on and off as we get to work. These principles hold true in more than just business settings. They can also be applied at home, in volunteer organizations, professional associations and in your place of worship.

Opera singer, Beverly Sills once observed that the best part about her job was that she *got* to do it rather than *having* to do it. Your ability as a leader to inspire others to look forward to doing their job is an essential element to maintaining and enhancing performance at all levels.

Pages 51 - 57 contain a selection of questions you should be asking about your employees. Remember that it is better to gather this information in an informal manner through observation. In asking employees directly, you may not obtain totally honest answers.

* * *

The **Two Minute Motivator** remembers that:

1. Every person has a different set of experiences, values and attitudes.

2. Any attempt to motivate someone must be filtered through what you know about them.

3. The elements which affect a person's motivation include external factors such as the other people in the working environment.

4. They also include internal factors such as the person's level of self-esteem.

5. How you, the supervisor, are viewed by your staff affects your ability to motivate them.

6. An essential key to motivation is to grasp two minute opportunities to ask questions and discover more about each individual.

Employee's Understanding of Job Content

* Does this person understand how their job fits into the organization?
* Do they have the skills required to complete the job successfully?
* Do they clearly understand your expectations of job performance?
* Do they know specifically how they will be evaluated?
* Do they understand where additional help and resources can be found?
* Do they know how their performance can both meet your expectations and exceed them?
* Do they feel they have been adequately trained to perform the job?

Employee's Observations of the Supervisor

* Does your employee believe you have an "open door" policy?

* Do they consider you approachable?

* How frequently do they formally evaluate your performance as their supervisor?

* How do they feel their comments about you are acknowledged?

* Do they believe you are a team leader?

* Do they have experience working with you in a project setting?

* How do they perceive your social skills?

* In what words would this person describe you as a person?

* How would they describe their own level of trust in you as a supervisor?

* How would they describe you as a role model within the organization?

* How would they evaluate your approach to rewarding positive behaviors? (Do they believe your approach is consistent?)

* How would they describe your overall style of supervision?

Employee's Values and Experience

* How would you go about determining your employee's values and ethics?

* What comments and actions have they made that are clues to their values?

* How would you describe their work ethic?

* How would you describe their level of integrity?

* Where did your employee work in the past?

* What attitudes did they experience in those settings?

* What responsibilities did they have?

* Why did your employee accept their present position?

* What education and training have they had?

* How closely matched are the duties in their present position with their training and education?

* Do they appear to be internally or externally motivated?

* How much do they rely on you for motivation/inspiration?

* How much do they rely on co-workers for motivation/inspiration?

* What particular areas of interest do they have on the job? Off the job?

* How do they perceive their present job fitting into the rest of their life?

* How do they help or hinder co-workers in completing their jobs?

* In what terms would you describe their level of investment in the job?

* In what ways do they exert additional effort where needed?

Environmental Factors Affecting the Employee

* What factors in the work setting makes your employee's job easier or harder to do?

* Are the proper resources available to help them to accomplish their job?

* How controlled does the employee feel in the work environment?

* How does the pace of work help or hinder your employee's ability to accomplish their job? (Volume of tasks, complexity of tasks, rate of change in tasks and responsibilities)

* What is the balance between quality and quantity of work?

* Does the organization provide a physically comfortable environment? (Ample work space, comfortable furniture, adequate lighting, level of noise, easy-to-use telephone system, etc.)

* What factors in the work setting help or hinder communication between employees and

between the organization and its customers?

* What factors in the work setting encourage or discourage your employee's trust?

* What are the signs of segregation between supervisors and non-supervisory employees? How do these factors help or hinder performance?

* How do you segregate yourself from those you supervise? How do each of these factors help or hinder your employee's performance?

People Factors Influencing the Employee

* How is a strong work ethic perceived by your employee?

* What influence do other employees have on this employee?

* In what terms would you describe the level of

trust among employees?

* What influence does this level of trust have on this employee?

* Under what circumstances does this employee "follow the crowd"?

* Under what circumstances does this person "avoid the crowd"?

* How likely is this person to participate in "group think"? And under what circumstances?

* * *

Exploring Your Values and Motivations

We spent the last chapter examining the elements which influence your staff's motivation. Now it is time to explore your own. What motivates you?

Your values and attitudes about how to inspire others depends on how you feel about yourself. While every staff member needs your leadership, how you motivate each one depends on how you feel about:
* That person
* Yourself
* Your job
* The organization

You may tend to pay special attention to the

Exploring Your Values and Motivations / 59

people you consider "rising stars." But as a supervisor, you must learn how to feel comfortable in your position to do so. On the other hand, if you perceive "rising stars" as threats, you might have second thoughts about encouraging them. In both cases, it is wise to look at your own feelings toward various staff members.

In another instance, you might try motivating an employee by talking about promotions because you value promotions. If the employee is more interested in spending more time with their family however, your strategy will fall on deaf ears.

Being in touch with the values that influence you and your behavior is critical to inspiring others. Keeping this in mind as well as remembering the elements that influence your staff members paints a clear picture of how you can spark others to perform as you wish they would.

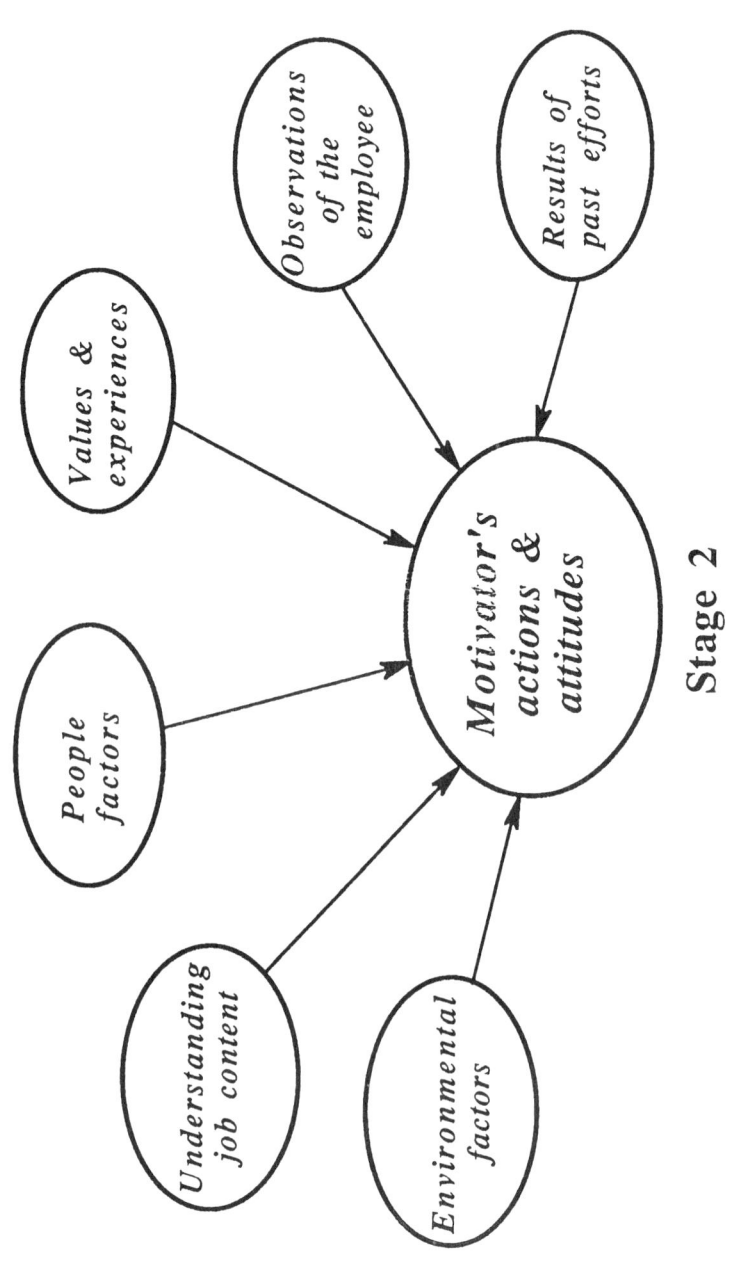

Factors Affecting Your Motivation

As you can see from the diagram on page 60, your motivation is influenced by the same motivational elements as those you supervise. When the information and insights from these factors are combined, they create your attitudes and emotions about your job, organization, and those with whom you work.

If you like your job, you will more naturally want to encourage and inspire others. When you dislike or have job-related problems, your mood will reflect this through your actions, comments and overall demeanor.

In spite of how you feel about your job from day-to-day, it is essential that you provide inspiration for those you supervise. Your ability to recognize how your values, background and emotions influence others will enable you to find the most effective ways to motivate them.

Exploring Your Motivational Biases

As you approach every opportunity to influence your people, a variety of thoughts will pass through your mind. Just as the people you are supervising use self-talk, you do to.

What does your self-talk say when you are trying to inspire another person? It might begin with a review of events such as, "Sandy seems to be stuck in a rut. She used to come up with so many suggestions. The past couple of weeks she's gotten awfully quiet."

Then your self-talk might wander to, "I remember when my employee, Ralph, blew up at that customer service problem last year. He'd been awfully quiet right before that. I wonder if there is something brewing with Sandy like there was with Ralph when he was so quiet."

And finally, it might suggest a strategy like, "Sandy has to meet with me tomorrow regarding the new uniforms. I think I'll poke around a little then. That way, she won't feel like she's being confronted without warning."

Throughout this internal discussion you're having with yourself, another internal conversa-

* * *

Being pro-active in motivating others is a critical element in inspiring superior performance.

* * *

tion may bring up issues related to you. This part of your underlying self-talk might say, "I get so tired of having to keep my eye on other people. Every time I turn around, somebody is having some kind of problem."

To a thought about about how Sandy might be ready to blow up, it might respond, "I don't want what Ralph did last year to happen again. That made me look really stupid!"

Finally, your self-talk might leave you with, "On the other hand, if I can get Sally really fired up again, it'll make me look real good. I wouldn't mind *that* pat on the back."

All through this secondary conversation, there is one common theme: WIIFM (What's in it for me?). This is a natural response. Most people are in the habit of thinking about themselves first. There is really nothing wrong with that. Some even call it a survival instinct. But people must balance their self-interest with consideration of others.

You cannot motivate someone without first being motivated yourself. Just as your staff needs to feel comfortable in their jobs, you need to feel comfortable in yours. Your job as a supervisor job is often more complex than that of your employees. But you share the same emotions and mental challenges as your employees.

If you feel frustrated about the way things are going, your mood and patience will fluctuate. If things are going well, you're apt to be more generous, happy and understanding with others.

As mentioned, the diagram on page 60 describes the elements involved with your own motivation and
your ability to motivate others. Once again, they are divided into external and internal factors.

* * *

External Factors

Just as each of your employees is influenced by internal and external factors, you are too. While you may view these factors from a different perspective, these elements contribute to your sense of confidence and self-esteem.

Your understanding of your employee's job content: Not only does each employee need to understand exactly what their jobs require, you must have a clear understanding as well.

Chances are, you are supervising at least one person whose job duties you have not performed. It is essential then that you know as much about that person's day-to-day activities as possible. Not only does this ease tension when this person is absent, but more importantly, it gives you a perspective on what they are going through. By understanding this, you will be better able to develop strategies to motivate this employee.

Even if you held this employee's position

in the past, chances are the day-to-day responsibilities have changed significantly. Ask questions to find out which job elements are the same, which are different and which are particularly challenging to the employee this time.

She might for instance, have to deal with a computerized version of what you used to do manually. For this reason, she may have more detail to cope with. Working to gain a new perspective on the employee's job also demonstrates that you care about her and what she does all day.

Work environment: For the most part you, as a supervisor, are affected by the same environmental factors as others in your organization. A broken toilet or lack of paper for the copier not only frustrates you as the person in charge, but it frustrates others too.

The major difference between you and those you supervise is that you have the power to alter your environment (or at least a portion of it). While you may not be able to have windows installed in a windowless office, you may be able

* * *

The major difference between you and those you supervise is that you have the power to alter your environment.

* * *

to have the walls repainted from dingy gray to bright yellow or white.

You also have the authority to change day-to-day routines that prove to be inefficient or cause tension among your staff. Eliminating unnecessary procedures for instance, can do much to motivate your entire staff (not to mention affecting the bottom line).

When you think about how to best motivate others, reflect on how the surrounding environment affects all of you. Do what you can to improve the working conditions and procedures that influence everyone in your organization.

People environment: Not only does the physical environment affect others, but the people environment also has an effect. If staff members insist on working individually instead of as a team, there may be problems you need to investigate. These interpersonal problems can have serious effects on people's attitudes and morale.

Just as you can influence the work environment you, as supervisor, can take steps to encourage healthy ways for people to interact with each other. The approach you take in trying to foster good relations among employees should be tied to the needs of the individuals in your organization. The more you are in touch with their desires and needs, the more you will be able to predict how they will react to the things you do.

Detecting discontentment over a particular policy and addressing that issue may not in itself improve motivation. But the fact that you were willing to discuss your staff's feelings about it may help them reduce their negative reaction to the policy.

As you attempt to motivate your people, remember that they may have the same concerns about working relationships as you do. Put yourself in their place and imagine what emotions they might have about the other people in the organization. Taking time to recognize these concerns with them will demonstrate that you are in touch with those in the work place. That fact in itself will help stimulate good will.

Results of past efforts to motivate: It is natural to expect that every person on your staff will need to be motivated from time to time. Sometimes you will succeed in your efforts; other times you may not.

For instance, you may have used a particular method to encourage an employee to improve her customer service skills. She responded positively for one week and then fell back into the same pattern she used before. In another situation, you noted that this same person made a complete change in her behavior and continued to demonstrate this change.

Why did she respond to one approach and not the other? What was different about the two attempts? Did you reason with her differently in one instance versus the other? Was she in a different mood during one instance?

While we cannot always predict why people do what they do, we can look back at their track record or general pattern of behavior. Make a note of what approach works with each member of your organization. Compare this information with other things you know about them.

You may have discovered for instance, that whenever your assistant starts to talk about cycling, he goes on forever. When you suggested he organize a company cycling club, he did not get excited, but he did get fired up about competing in a city-wide cycling contest.

In examining the differences between these two related ideas more closely, you may discover that he thrives on competiton but detests organization. Perhaps this is the reason for his less than acceptable work at maintaining reports. What can you do now that you have made this discovery?

By using these techniques, you will be better able to predict how best to motivate each person on your staff.

* * *

Being in touch with your own motivation is essential to inspiring others.

* * *

Internal Factors

Values and background: As is true with every person you supervise, your own values and experiences influence the actions you take. Some of your experiences add to your skills as a supervisor, while others may detract from them.

You may learn over time for instance, that listening is a much more effective supervisory skill, than is talking. At the same time, these same experiences may have made you impatient with "inane co-workers who can't get anything right the first four times!"

While this example may be an exaggeration, it demonstrates how each experience can be interpreted in a number of ways. Your ability to apply the best of these lessons will help make you a more effective motivator.

The factors we have covered while trying to better understand those you supervise are the same ones you must take into consideration for yourself. Gaining perspective on how these same elements affect you in your working relationships will provide the insight you need to locate the

* * *

By using these techniques, you will be better able to predict how best to motivate each person on your staff.

* * *

most effective motivational triggers.

Your formal education for instance, may have stopped after two years of college. Yet you are supervising people who, in some cases, have attained masters' degrees in their fields.

While day-to-day conversation may not reflect it, you might feel intimidated by their level of education. Perhaps you even feel frustrated that you never finished your degree.

Yet you may also have five years of management experience while your co-workers have just entered the work force. Being able to keep feelings about your formal education in focus is essential to your ability to think clearly about how to motivate these individuals. For all you know, they may be concerned about their lack of management experience and are looking to you for inspiration.

In another instance, you may be of Hispanic heritage. The primary language spoken while you were growing up might have been Spanish. As a result it is possible you are self-conscious about your accent.

While you are an experienced manager

who was promoted on your merit, there might be someone in your department who feels favoritism played a role. How do you find ways to motivate someone with this attitude? (You might begin by determining whether the person in question actually feels this way?)

In a third situation, you might be 24 years old while those you supervise are as much as 30 years your senior. You know you are fully capable of doing your job, but you get the feeling others may not take you seriously.

What can you do to motivate co-workers old enough to be your father? Upon investigating, you might discover that some are happy to have a supervisor with some youth and energy in the department. Or you might discover that for some, simply asking their advice and counsel will inspire them because of their feeling of a need to contribute.

Examining your values and experiences as they relate to those you supervise will always provide some insights for finding new inspiration.

Observing Employees

It is your job as supervisor to observe people's actions every day. But to effectively motivate each individual, you must look a level deeper than at just their behavior.

One person may be able to maintain an acceptable performance and yet hate their job. Another might appear to be having the best time in the world but is not meeting even your most minimal expectations. While you are not expected to be a mind reader, each person's non-verbal communication will reveal most of what you need to know.

Consider the people you presently supervise. Which ones have consistently been your best performers? What have they done which makes you feel that way? Is it that they meet your expectations? Or that they take the initiative? Do they always seem to "save the day"? And what have you done to encourage them?

Now consider those who are not meeting your expectations. What traits, if any, do they all have in common? What are they doing (or not doing) which makes them poor performers? How have you tried to motivate each one of them?

The big question in motivation is "why?" Why are some people motivated while others are not? Why do motivational strategies work with some people but not with others?

The more you know about each individual with whom you work, the better you will be able to answer these questions. Here are a few tips to observe each day:

Keep an eye on body language. The vast majority of what we communicate is done non-verbally. This includes facial expressions, eye contact, posture, hand motions, level of enthusiasm, the way someone walks.

Listen to more than just what the person says. How are they saying it? What tone of voice are they using? How much are they participating in conversations and meetings? How confident is their voice?

Examine this person's track record? What topics really get them excited or interested? Which topics do they avoid? Are there issues which anger them? How do they interact with others?

Test your assumptions. If your employee appears upset, ask her about it. She may say, "no!" But then you know for sure. Or if someone seems depressed or frustrated, investigate the situation. Drawing conclusions without having the facts can prove to be one of the biggest de-motivators of all.

Understanding what motivates you and how you feel about your own job and the people you supervise is essential to helping you develop a consistent style of inspiration for others. Your ability to anticipate and respond to their needs demonstrates how much you care for each individual you supervise.

Consult pages 82 -87 for a more complete list of questions to ask about yourself about your values and motivations.

The **Two Minute Motivator** remembers that:

1. Attitudes about motivating others depend on how you feel about yourself.

2. Every time you try to motivate someone, your behavior is influenced by your own biases.

3. You need to make an effort to clearly understand the scope of each of your employees' jobs.

4. When trying to motivate someone, think back about which methods have worked in the past.

5. Personal values will influence your perception of others.

6. Making assumptions is usually counterproductive when motivating others.

7. Looking deeper than a person's behavior helps you to discover what is motivating them.

Motivator's Values and Experiences

* How well matched are your job responsibilities with your formal education and training?
* How well matched is your previous work experience with your present job duties?
* How well do your values and work ethic fit into your job?
* How much do you rely on others for motivation/inspiration?
* Describe your level of interest in supervising and motivating others in relation to the other duties in your job.
* How does your job fit into your life balance? (eg. work to live vs. live to work?)
* Why did you accept your position?
* What are your aspirations for your position?
* What motivates you to do a better job?
* What factors in your job make you feel uncomfortable?

* How does your level of comfort in supervising your employees influence your ability to motivate them?

Motivator's Observations of the Employee

* Does your employee complete work on time?
* Do they produce quality work?
* Do they provide input and suggestions for improvement?
* Do they volunteer for extra projects?
* Do they initiate work?
* How much training/instruction do they generally require?
* How much coaching do they generally require? What kind of coaching?
* How do they demonstrate their level of trust in you as a supervisor?
* How do they show their enthusiasm for their job?

* How do they demonstrate their cooperation in working with others?

* What projects and/or tasks get them excited?

* How do they demonstrate that they feel motivated?

* Describe your level of comfort in motivating this employee.

Environmental Factors Influencing the Motivator

* What factors in the work setting make your job easier or harder to do?

* Are the proper resources available for you to accomplish your job?

* How controlled do you feel by the environment?

* How does the pace of work help or hinder you in accomplishing your job? (Volume of tasks, complexity of tasks, rate of change in tasks and responsibilities, etc.)

* What is the balance between quality and quantity of work in your job?

* Does the organization provide a physically comfortable environment? (Ample work space, comfortable furniture, adequate lighting, level of noise, easy-to-use telephone system, etc.)

* What factors in the work setting help or hinder communication between employees and between the organization and its customers?

* What factors in the work setting encourage or discourage employee trust?

* What are the signs of segregation between supervisors and non-supervisory employees? How do these factors help or hinder your performance?

* How do you segregate yourself from those you supervise? How do each of these factors help or hinder your performance?

Results of Past Efforts to Motivate the Employee

* How do you define motivational reward (your opportunities to acknowledge and encourage positive behaviors in your employees)?

* Have you rewarded this employee in the past?

* What techniques have worked? Why?

* What techniques have not worked? Why?

* How do you tailor motivational rewards to this employee?

* How do you elicit their input about motivational rewards?

* How do you know when you have been effective?

* What do you do to encourage this employee's motivation?

* Does what you do help promote this employee?

* How do you determine an effective reward structure for them?

Motivator's Understanding of the Employee's Job Content

* Have you served in this employee's position?

* Describe your understanding of their job duties and how they fit into the overall organizational structure.

* Describe your understanding of performance expectations for this employee's job.

* In what terms would you describe this position's influence on the organization?

* In what terms would you describe the organization's influence on this position?

 ## Inspiring Motivation in Others

Inspiring motivation in others is both an opportunity and a risk. If you succeed in motivating an individual, you will also arouse their increased interest and productivity. If you fail to motivate them, you run the risk of losing your effectiveness as a supervisor.

Motivating others contains three major elements:

* The attitudes and values of the person you are trying to motivate.
* Your own attitudes and values.
* The person's reaction to your attempts to motivate them.

We have already covered these first two

elements in chapters two and three, but now it's time to explore the third: the person's reaction to your attempts to motivate them.

As you examine what motivates you and others, a variety of ideas will come to your mind about how to approach different situations. Every individual you work with will present a different series of challenges to your ability to motivate them.

Some of your top performers for example, might tire of routine work very quickly. Your major challenge with them is to provide new stimulation.

Your marginal performers will probably require more one-on-one attention to help maintain their focus and attention to detail. Your consistent performers, or those who make up the backbone of the organization, will probably require your regular support and encouragement.

Each person within the organization is above

all, an individual, even though they may fit into one of these three categories. Once you are tuned into their values and their sense of self-motivation, you will need to find consistent ways of encouraging them.

The three or four individuals who form the backbone of your staff are each motivated in different ways. While they all will most likely respond to attempts at team building, each has certain needs which, when met, will trigger their internal sense of inspiration.

One employee may be extremely devoted to his family. Therefore, asking about his family or perhaps sharing about your family, may encourage his sense of belonging and self-esteem.

Another employee might be an avid football fan. Asking her about who's going to win the Superbowl on the opening day of training camps may show her you care about her as a person.

A third employee may be pursuing a business degree at night. By periodically sharing how you juggle your management and budgeting responsibilities, you may inspire this person to work even harder. (In this case, lending support and understanding during exam time will also go a long way to building good will.)

As you attempt to motivate each person on your staff, three elements require your consideration. As you can see from the diagram on page 92, every person is evaluating your attempts to motivate them from several different angles.

This evaluation once again comes in the form of self-talk. This means the mental voice provides facts, biases, background and predictions, or a sort of "play-by-play" analysis of what could happen. The three elements you must consider are:

* The person's orientation toward change
* The person's perception of what other people will think or say.
* How this attempt at motivation impacts the person's values.

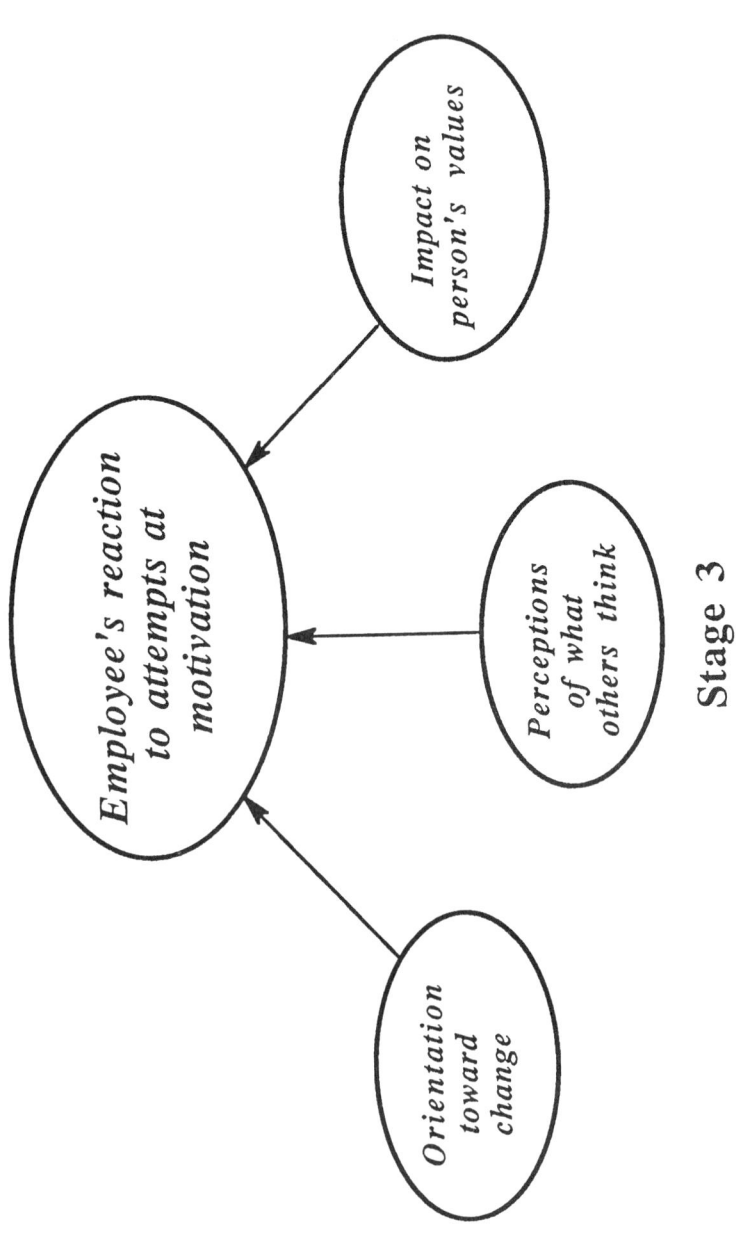

The person's orientation toward change.

How comfortable does this person feel with change? Are they set in their ways? Or are they flexible? Do they look forward to new ways of doing things?

Some of your attempts to motivate may not require a significant change of behavior. Buying an employee a cup of coffee or talking sports for instance, may encourage their sense of well-being. And these things do not require a change in behavior.

On the other hand, you may seek out his thoughts on a better way to process orders. If he is open to change, he will probably jump at the chance to exert some influence. However, if he is comfortable in his "rut," he may simply provide some marginal input just to satisfy your questions. And unless you pursue the issue, he will probably forget it ever came up.

Understanding a person's orientation to change before you make an attempt to motivate them is a key predictor to your success. This leads us to your second consideration:

The person's perception of what other people will think or say.

Most of the way your workers evaluate this element comes through their self-talk which is based on their experiences both inside and outside the work place.

You may for example, begin delegating additional tasks to a particular person because you know she enjoys doing them. While she may be appreciative of your efforts, she might also be concerned about what her co-workers will think.

Her self-talk might go something like this:

"Rob's really making an attempt to follow through on his promises to delegate new responsibilities to me. What he's given me will provide some great experience.

"But what will my co-workers think? I saw how they razed Betty when she got that promotion. Am I in for the same treatment? After all, I party with these people after work! I know it is in my best interests to take on new tasks, but maybe I'm not ready for all this."

As you can see, even your best of intentions to help an employee can be thwarted by their assumptions and fears. By taking the time to anticipate an employee's apprehensions you, as supervisor, can work to help the employee overcome them.

You might say, "I know you enjoy being one of the gang out there. I also know that you have a real desire to learn this part of the job. How do you think we should approach this?"

By asking for the employee's feedback, you are demonstrating your concern about her place in the group. At the same time, you can gain additional insight about what motivates her.

Some people are more concerned about appearances than others. It is your responsibility as a motivator to take these issues into consideration. The third element you must consider is:

How this attempt at motivation impacts this person's values.

Values play a large role in determining whether a person will respond to your motiva-

*   *   *

By asking for the employee's feedback, you are demonstrating your concern about their place in the group.

*   *   *

tional attempts. When factors such as a person's conscience, emotions and sense of fairness come into play, they may sometimes override the person's resistance to change or concern about what others may think.

A marginal worker for example, may respond to your suggestions about getting more done because, deep down, he knows he is hindering productivity. He may be a very loyal worker who is stuck in a rut. He may also be the party organizer in the department.

Yet if you anticipate these concerns, you may be able to build a motivational rapport that will enhance this worker's productivity and keep him productive. You might begin by asking about the next party coming up. Does he have enough help in organizing it? Can you help in any way?

From there, you might mention your "concern" about his slipping productivity and how it is having an impact on everyone.

He will probably say something like, "Yeah, I know. Sometimes I get a little distracted. I've been doing this for so long, there's nothing challenging about it."

You might respond, "I've watched you do great work in the past. What can we do to make your job more interesting?"

At this point, his self-talk may be, "She's right. I have been marking time. But I'm comfortable where I am and there are all these great people around. What would they think if I suddenly started being a high-producing, straight-arrow kind of guy?

"On the other hand, maybe that is what they're waiting for. I really haven't been pulling my weight. I need to get my act in gear."

From here, you will probably see a substantial improvement in this person's productivity. But, motivation does not stop here. If he comes up with suggestions for making his job more interesting, act on them. If he starts to slip, remind him of how much everyone is counting on his participation and, don't forget to compliment him on his party organizing skills.

Once your attempt to motivate an employee takes place, two events occur. First, the employee records your attempt to motivate them and their own response. They will use this information again when responding to your future attempts at motivation. This information, pleasant or unpleasant, becomes part of the person's values and background, and is critical to their sense of motivation.

Second, you are also recording the person's reaction to your attempt so you may use the information when you need to motivate this person again. Over a period of time, these actions and reactions will develop into a track record. By using this record, you can establish a basis from which to motivate this person in the future.

For each of the three elements we have just considered, a list of questions has been provided on pages 101 through 103. Now that you understand **Two Minute Motivation**, it is time to put it to work!

* * *

The **Two Minute Motivator** remembers that:

1. Inspiring motivation is both an opportunity and a risk.

2. Many attempts at motivation do not require significant changes in behavior.

3. Understanding the person's feelings about change is a key factor to predicting your success in motivating them.

4. A person's perception of what others will think is crucial element in motivation.

5. Impacting a person's values will sometimes override resistance to change and what others think.

6. Effective motivation requires consistent follow-up and encouragement.

Employee's Orientation Toward Change

* How flexible is this employee?

* How open to suggestions are they?

* How do they approach new opportunities?

* Describe the support this employee needs to make a substantial change? (in position duties, work setting, level of responsibilities, etc.)

* How do they generally perceive change in the organization?

* When this employee is uncomfortable with a change, how do they react?

* In what cases have you observed this person welcoming change?

* How do they view change outside of work?

Employee's Perception of What Other People Think

* How does this employee think the organization's management feels about employee motivation?

* How subject are they to peer pressure?

* What in the organization's culture blocks attempts at motivation?

* Where does this person fit into the natural leadership of the organization? (leader or follower, under whose influence?)

* What attitudes does the organization's culture have about employee motivation?

* Which of these attitudes help and what can be done to encourage them?)

*Which of these attitudes hinder and what can be done to discourage them?)

How the Motivational Strategy Impacts the Employee's Values

* How does the strategy address this employee's values and background?

* How effective is the strategy for this employee based on what you have learned about them?

* What do you expect from your employee as a result of using this strategy?

* How can you capitalize on using this strategy if it works?

Putting the Two Minute Motivator to Work

Let's review what we've learned so far. *Two Minute Motivation* is based on three elements:

* The attitudes and values of the person you are trying to motivate.
* Your own attitudes and values.
* The person's reaction to your attempts to motivate them.

We know that every person's motivation in the work place depends on five factors including their:

* Job content
* Personal values and experiences
* Physical environment

* Perceptions of their co-workers and
* Observations about the person motivating them

We also know that your actions as a motivator depend on six factors including your:
* Understanding of their job content
* Observations about them
* Personal values and experiences
* Physical environment
* Perceptions of co-workers and
* Results of your past efforts to motivate.

Finally, we know that your employees' reactions to motivation depend on three factors including:
* Their orientation toward change
* Their perceptions of what others will think and
* The impact your attempt to motivate them has on their values

But how can you put this process to work on a day-to-day basis?

Putting the Two Minute Motivator to Work

Diagram: Two Minute Motivation

Stage 1 — Employee's Attitudes: Observations of motivator, Values & experiences, Job content, Environment factors, People factors

Stage 2 — Motivator's Attitudes: Values & experiences, Observations of employee, Past efforts, People, Job content, Environment factors

Stage 3 — Employee's Reaction: Impact on values, What others think, Change

© Copyright 1991 Robert W. Wendover -- All rights reserved

Motivation is not just talk. It is also action. And modeling. It is setting an example for others to see. Your level of enthusiasm and motivation has a direct impact on the motivation, enthusiasm and vigor of others.

In attempting to motivate someone, ask yourself three questions:

1. What are my values? What do I want to get out of this for myself? What do I want to see accomplished?

2. What are the other person's values?

3. How can I combine my values with my employee's values to better motivate them?

The phrase "walking your talk" holds true in the motivation of others more than anywhere else.

* * *

Your day-to-day tasks revolve around a series of situations. You can anticipate how someone will react to your attempts to motivate them by developing a better understanding of how they think. Even the way the day starts may be greatly influenced by the way your employees enter the work place. If they come in anticipating a problem with you, they will already be on their guard.

Think about the atmosphere in the office as weather. How would you describe it? It is cloudy? Partly sunny? Stormy? You might ask others how they feel about the atmosphere in the office. While some may be reluctant to reveal their true feelings, over a period of time they may express emotions or make suggestions that provide keys to creating a more motivational atmosphere.

Sometimes it's the little comments overheard at the coffee machine which can reveal the most about what people are thinking about their jobs.

Increase your awareness about the present work environment and how people are feeling every day. You can accomplish this not only by asking them, but more importantly by observing what they say and their non-verbals and behaviors.

Keeping track of this information and reviewing it when you are looking for opportunities to motivate someone is an organized way to help you inspire them.

You can gather this information in a number of settings. Consider the following:

General office environment: What does the employee say to others while working? How do they react to others' comments? What makes them bristle? What do they find amusing? What off-hand comments do they make which may lead you to detect their underlying values? Are they a loner or do they often seek social contact with others?

Work habits: How well do they concentrate? Do they get the job done on time? Do they meet your expectations? How much training time or verbal direction do they need? How many questions do they ask? Are they willing to take risks to get the job done? Are they enthusiastic about the skills and abilities they are using?

Meetings: Do they participate? How do they participate? Are they a leader? Do they speak first or last? Do they have a reputation for a particular type of behavior in meetings such as making funny or caustic comments? Do they look to others for leadership? Are they independent in their way of thinking?

Social gatherings: Do they participate? How do they participate? Are they a natural leader? What is the nature of their comments? Do they have fun? How do they appear to feel about others? Are there subjects they tend to avoid? Are there subjects which dominate their conversations?

One-on-one conversations: Do they appear intimidated by you as a manager? Are they concerned about your perception of their performance? Are they comfortable in your presence? Do they feel free to make comments and contributions for the "cause"? Do they bristle at particular references especially those referring to their abilities, skills, education, age, culture and ethnicity, etc.?

In all of these job-related settings, it is wise to observe more than just the spoken word. Look for changes in voice inflection, manner of speaking, posture, eye contact, facial expressions, appearance and level of confidence.

As you observe people, take a few seconds to assess the environment. Ask open-ended questions and investigate. Are they anticipating your moves? Do they share your enthusiasm?

If you choose to delegate a project, make sure the individual is interested in doing it. If they aren't, ask why and then try to sell the benefits. Simply delegating something because you are in charge will not result in the best outcome. Ask about their concerns. They may fear they cannot handle the project and, for that reason, may resist it.

Can the project be modified to fit their

* * *

Ask.

Listen.

Learn.

* * *

values? Can certain tasks be assigned to someone else who is stronger in that area? While this takes more effort on your part, the resulting enthusiasm is more than worth the result.

Finally, give your employees enough information to make good decisions. Knowledge is power and withholding knowledge from others discourages them from attacking their jobs with vigor.

These techniques do not have to be confined to a place of business. Some of the finest areas to help others develop are through professional associations, places of worship, social clubs and other volunteer organizations. As a volunteer leader in these places, you might consider polishing some of your motivational skills before you use them on the job. Encourage others to do the same.

Too often, we engage in the art of competitive listening where we inflict our values on others by interrupting them. By not being able to fully express their thoughts, people may feel a sense of frustration and impatience. Being listened to is one of the most powerful motivators around.

However, we tend to anticipate and finish other people's sentences for them. The temptation of course, is to hear only what we choose to hear instead of listening to the person's entire message.

Listen, listen, listen, and you will learn, learn, learn. Use silence as an opportunity to get individuals to reveal more about themselves. Since most people find silence uncomfortable, waiting an extra second before you speak again may elicit another comment from them. You'll gain more insight into what the person is thinking.

A key to implementing any motivational strategy is to find out what the the person needs and to respond to that desire. Motivators also need to be willing to take chances. Just as a good manager takes chances in order to accomplish a particular task, a good motivator must be willing to take some chances to discover what really makes a person value their work.

The key to motivating an employee is to

find a match between your motivational strategy and that person's values. You must overcome any obstacles to their motivaiton. These include repeated interruptions, noise distractions, physical obstacles in the working environment and office politics among others.

You must maintain your focus when trying to motivate that particular individual. While you may supervise a number of people, your strategies for each one must be tailored to each person's needs and values.

The support you give must be unconditional based on what your people need, not on what you want them to need. And the better you know your employees, the easier it will be to create ways to provide two minute opportunities for motivation.

Motivation does not mean creating cash incentives (though money can help motivate people). In this case, it means giving people the opportunity to express themselves and to feel a sense of accomplishment, contribution and value.

Following through and being consistent when motivating people is paramount for inspir-

* * *

Listen, listen, listen

and you will

learn, learn, learn.

* * *

ing them. You must be willing to do what you say you'll do. Once you have committed to a particular motivational strategy, make sure you complete it. Do not change your plan mid-way through. If you do, you will only reverse any positive effects you began and, in essence, de-motivate your people.

Setting goals is a good example of this. On a periodic basis, most employees set goals when their supervisor asks them to. Yet many supervisors fail to extend continued support to their employees as they attempt to accomplish their goals. Your ability to follow through to assist your people in achieving their goals can be one of the most important steps in beginning to better motivate them.

Meet each person on your staff where they are in their development on the job. In many cases, a lack of self-esteem is a major obstacle to motivation. Your ability to help your people understand that they are okay as they are now, but that they can grow to be more valuable and to contribute and accomplish more in the future is essential.

As you begin to implement a motivational strategy for each individual, ask yourself a set of filter questions to help you determine whether your strategy will be effective:

1. Is this strategy serving me or serving them?
2. Does this plan keep their overall values in mind?
3. Will my people understand the purpose of my strategy?
4. Is my plan consistent with other efforts I have made to motivate my employees?

By asking yourself these four questions, you'll discover whether your plan will be effective for the individual you designed it for.

* * *

Recognize the subtle ways motivation takes place. You may for instance, encourage someone to take on a particular project because you feel it would be good for their career. And out of respect for you, or because they report to you, that person may go out and complete the project, even though they have no interest in it.

That person might say, "yes" to you and "no" to themselves.

As a result, you might react with frustration when your employee responds with less enthusiasm than you would expect. Having a clearer picture of the person's values, desires and goals based on the two minute opportunities you use to observe them will help you tremendously.

Comments such as "Thank God, it's Friday" or "I'm glad it's hump day," are telling signs that someone is not enjoying their work as much as they could. People who arrive early and leave late may be conscientious about their position. Or, they may be feeling overwhelmed. Don't assume which it is. Instead, ask. Observe. And respond. It is your job as a motivator to discover how you can best help this individual.

In addition to the immediate pat on the back and words of support you give them, you should also create a list for each individual of the other creative techniques you can use to motivate them. Remember that motivation takes place in two to three minute opportunities. Therefore, your ability to respond quickly to something a person has done is crucial.

While pats on the back and words of encouragement during staff meetings are important, they don't come close to the consistent encouragement and cheerleading that people must have on a regular basis.

Develop a file of ideas as you come across them in your reading and interactions with others. What can you use to better work with those you supervise?

Once again, as you prepare to use each one of your ideas, run them through the four question filter we have already discussed. Be willing to take a chance with some unusual or offbeat ideas that will capture your people's attention and demonstrate that you are in touch with their values.

Fill your head with these two minute options. Create a mental file that you can use immediately. If you wait 24 hours before you pat someone on the back, it is often too late to do the most good.

Your ability to discover what a person is really thinking is the key to understanding how to adjust your motivational style to fit their needs.

Continually seek and evaluate the formal and informal feedback you receive from your employees. What are they thinking? Do they like what you are doing? Taking two minute opportunities to better understand your people and their values gives you essential information about what motivates them.

You cannot be too predictable however. Using the same motivational strategy over and over, will encourage cynicism. Consistency plus creativity, if nothing else, demonstrates your trust and your belief in each individual. Actions always speak louder than words.

Finally, seize the moment. Don't miss your opportunities to motivate people by putting them off until tomorrow. Don't let distractions get to you. Become more aware of the two minute chances you have each day to motivate your people. When you develop this into a regular pattern of behavior, you'll be amazed at how productive your people will become.

The **Two Minute Motivator** remembers that:

1. You anticipate the reactions of others by understanding how they are motivated.

2. Little comments can be the most revealing about how a person thinks.

3. When you observe people, you should also evaluate the surrounding environment.

4. If you listen, listen, listen, you will learn, learn, learn!

5. Motivation is giving every person an opportunity to express themselves and feel a sense of accomplishment.

6. Follow through and consistency are paramount for effective motivation.

7. Seizing the moment to provide encouragement will always be the best way to motivate.

* * *

Seize the moment to motivate!

* * *

Acknowledgements

So many people have contributed to this book through their ideas, support, love and good humor. But special appreciation goes to:

Okie Arnot, Geri Bell, Troy Campbell, Brian Legget, Hillard Rest, Marty Tarabar, and Glen Yandell for their review of the content.

Gene Drumm for helping me to hammer out the model of Two Minute Motivation.

Karen Saunders for her splendid cover design and technical support.

Diane Lewis for her accurate editing.

My many colleagues and clients who have provided two minute motivations for me on a constant basis!

And *Wendy Elliott Wendover,* my own *two minute motivator!*

Robert W. Wendover
Englewood, Colorado

Robert Wendover is the

Two Minute Motivator!

After nearly ten years of advising top companies on how to motivate employees, Robert Wendover now offers you his dynamic principles.

Bob is the author of **Smart Hiring**: *The Complete Guide for Recruiting Employees* and **High Performance Hiring**. His work has appeared in such prestigious publications as T*he Kiplinger Washington Letter*, the *American Management Association's President's Letter, Supervisory Management, Information Management*, the *National Business Employment Weekly* and a host of industry publications. He is a contributor to the *ManagersEdge* audio cassette program heard monthly by over 14,000 managers.

Robert Wendover has shared his insights with thousands of companies and agencies such as AT&T, US West, Hampton Inns, Piggly Wiggly Stores, the United States Army and Navy, and the State of Colorado.